re: verbs

praise for re: verbs

"I was Robert Swereda's creative writing teacher, but he didn't need me. I don't know why he stuck around as long as he did. These poems are what you can't be taught. Maybe he took note of Dorothy Trujillo Lusk's ambition to write unteachable poems. Possibly he enjoyed the consternation and confusion that Louis Cabri's poems produced in the other students. He was writing like this almost from the beginning. He was remarkably patient as he hung around waiting to hand in something like ***arpeggios on Leo Brouwer****. It made me wonder."*

~ Reg Johanson

"Filling storms within our memories, or turning the weather into our organs, Robert Swereda's ***re: verbs*** *pits human function against nature that expertly bends/blends the two lexicons. Robert Swereda is proving that in everything he writes, language is the focus, and all the ways in which we can push it/pull it/break it/fix it/change it/mash it/re-mix it."*

~ Daniel Zomparelli, editor-in-chief of Poetry Is Dead

re: verbs

Robert Swereda

BareBackPress

BareBackPress
Hamilton, Ontario, Canada
For enquires visit www.barebackpress.com
Contact BareBackPress at press@barebacklit.com
Cover layout by Choi Yunnam

ISBN-13: 978-0988075054
ISBN-10: 0988075059

Acknowledgements:

I would like to express gratitude to The Filling Station collective, vitamin B, friends back in Vancouver, Advil Cold & Sinus, Reg Johanson, people with couches I have slept on, and Fernet Branca.

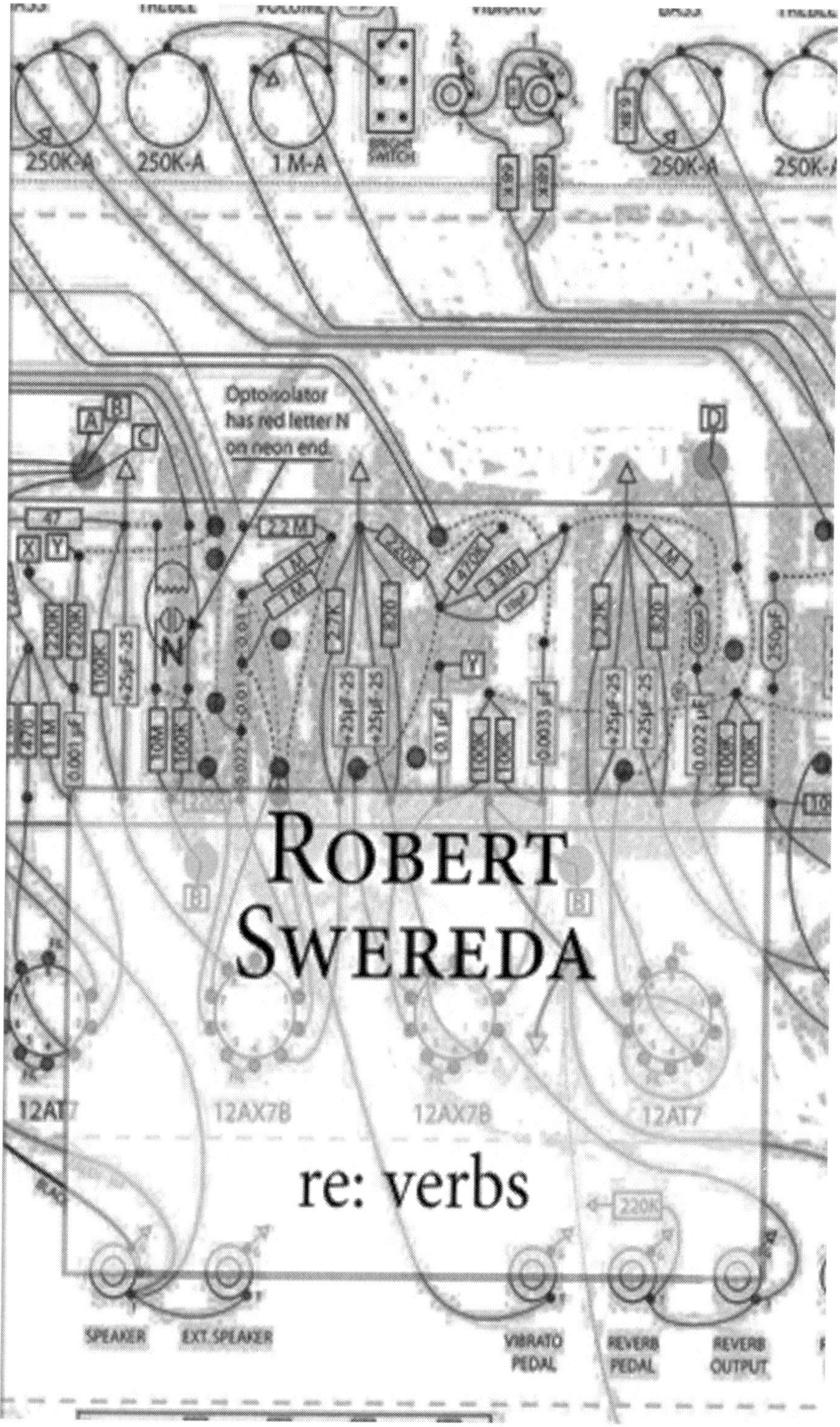
250K-A
250K-A
1 M-A
250K-A
Optoisolator
has red letter N
on neon end.
12AT7
12AX7B
12AX7B
12AT7
SPEAKER
EXT.SPEAKER
VIBRATO
PEDAL
REVERB
PEDAL
REVERB
OUTPUT

Robert Swereda

re: verbs

contents

verbs to be

arpeggios on Leo Brouwer

b)rainstorms

rvr vlly

currents

uninstalled

arson hearts

illegible seasons

verbs to be

sturdy. dying sport. roots recede back
to yesterday's picture.
heads the phase amusing

soft word to turn away with
in disruption

(hope) with sharp tongue.

tread amid noise, pending
c)or/chi/d
                    crown snap. desolate

frost loving clamour steep
into throat - primrose with grey

     I know,
          ect.

animal function in perpetual abeyance
subject to holding

overcoming doubt break of pallid face
and glazed eye
never did a boundary thirst.

robust tectonic *formal fit*
muscular panel pragmatic response to
need and circumstance

jilted band ground cracks

believed fresh

shine in curb knife squeeze out title

fidelity outward large turn
own genomic

evoking substance
visual
leaking disaster

adjusting wish to carve out
point of breaking thru the longer

                                line of vanity
cl | over.h.eard | rum[aging
                                jesters lie low

                        entry.
                        learn it now.

allow rogue thirst
hampering increase to bare-bone finesse

rumour eating dampness dawn
episode slips
stolen host. gently.

guilt. abridged

modelled on blend rival between notes
dangle uncertain

infernal.
still ambiguous
assembled to respect

bloated rime
draped over molten shoulders

pleasure sp i/e ll
archived in a round shatter
of places we're drawn to

.butchered

shield of skin

excused move   ros)eh(ip | honing

blank star(e) fumble

nature of gathering into mouths
warn of ruptured verbs

projected and kicking grace

factory for sewn surrender
employing bondage of memory fuses
drops subtle aviation on displacement

you've become a dangerous pattern of gratitude

dampening. moulding over.

the bond is thick and you disappear

clinging to a theatrical romp
an audience unfolding
reminding
of tearing truths

running on my abandoning idea of distance.

assumptions mix
into an atmosphere

mustang-thin: dealt out of
phase

holding in your lungs whirlpool traffic
from the larger patterns in which we've embedded desperate
composition

housed in audio duplex

charming glimpse kick-start elaborate heading

dismal titles to trample on

pebbles of word
pacing back and forth

to form exit strategy

throwing nets into droves of curse wide mouth
chasing minutes of demeaning charm

positioning into form inability
disruptive landscape reveal image
of temporal disunity - function puts
a frame around memory to provoke

(un)clot.t.(h)ed

a certain slant in speech
deprived of awareness. fashioned scale

rapid brush strokes with misguided
distance .imposing

arpeggios on Leo Brouwer

austere
/
bolted - obstructed - stuffy - strict
|
shut in
|
encirclement - hold
\
embrace
\
caress society
\ |
fondle - stroke movement
\ |
tone of voice - accent - cadence progression
| \ |
twang rhythm decline
\ |
pulsation drop
\ |
pounding -beating - loss dribble
\ |
outflow drip
\ |
mix up - muddle - shambles - fiasco - debacle - miscarriage *leakage*
| \ \
assembly - conclave influence - power failure **Fuga No. 1**
| \ / |
council blackout - *fugue* *fleeing*
|
absconding
/
in flight
/
miserable running off - breakout
\ |
down to earth - pragmatic - practical
/ \
feathers dirt - loam
|
scandal

score - scratch - mark of respect - tribute | frisk - inspect - check - try out - obtainable

worship - adoration - exaltation - *eulogy* | *skip* - cut - saw - aphorism - cliché - facile

elogio de la danza

obligation - appreciation - approval - *praise* | *caper* - jape - trick - skill - flair - gift

graffiti - lettering - scribble - hand - applause | prance - flounce - storm - gale - tempest

inception cockcrow
\ /
dawn on
\
strike - stop work
/
lash relation
\ /
slate - chalk - draw - tie- photo finish
|
censure sound bite - clip - mow - harvest
\ | \
disapproval - tartness yield
|
veer return
| |
bargain - wheel and deal bringing up the rear knock back
| \ |
opportunity orifice - vent - find expression for come down with
| / |
opening connoisseur - buff contract
| / |
introduction *overture* - taster *laconic* - curt - blunt - diminish
\ | /
foreword - **preludios epigramaticos**

Rito de los Orisha

/ \

stomach. *ceremony. routine.*

/ \ | | \

gut. bear out. service. sequence. custom.

/ \ \ / / |

intuitive. ransack. verify. - support. - assistance. chain. pattern.

/ |

immobilize. mold.

/ |

coarse. - gross. arrest. mildew.

/ | / |

abrasive. take in for questioning. growth.

\ |

brusque. probe.

|

lose the thread. - wander. explore.

/ \ |

edge through. get the drift. - see the sights.

circulate.- release. - spare.
\
hail. - snow. - static. - stationary. - frozen.   in excess of.
/   \   \
welcome. wedge. - lock. - *ringlet.*   sedated.   tip over.
| | | \   \
relaxed.   sliver.   **La Espiral eterna**   keep under wraps.   upset.
| \   / |
cozy.   flake. - peel. - rind. - coat. - conceal.   antagonize.
\   /
intimate. - confidential. - close. - just around the corner. - confront.

Ojos Brujos

/ \
screen jinx
| | \
monitor bugaboo spell
| |
keep an eye on interlude
/ |
adhere to pause in action
/ |
shadow skirmish
| |
eclipse scrap
| / \
overwhelm write off crumb
| \
annihilate sour
| /
beat ferment
/ \ /
dog-tired. punch tumult
| \
pizzazz chauffer hullabaloo
/ | /
spark drive into din
\ \ /
trigger ship instil
| \ /
spur vessel pour
| \ /
goad media bucket
\ /
badger - press - bear down on
\
stomach

pulp rider
| /
in the flesh proviso
| /
vogue immerse yourself caveat
/ / /
fad bathe warning
/ / /
fashion dip hint
/ | |
whittle saddle with finishing touch to
/ / /
carve handicap crown
/ / /
slice minus trophy
/ / /
Piezas Sin Titulo

Variations On A Theme

/ | \

ups and downs taking place argument

| | |

lea whereabouts row

| | \ \

field locus punt take the oars

| / \ |

line of work socket posture blade

| | | |

parentage hollow ham it up fin

| | |

background lay it on thick appendage

| | /

milieu unqualified accessory

| | /

climate utter auxiliary

| | /

mood emit garnish

| | /

humour release gravy

pigheaded
|
inflexible shakeup
| |
set perturb
| |
reredos trouble
| |
backcloth woe
| |
Paisaje Cubano Con Tristeza
/
on the team
|
fib slouch panel
\ / |
lie plate
/ / |
loll salver overlay
/ / |
sag dish intersection
| / |
punctuation drop distribute node
\ | / |
dash - scatter burl

put under somebody's nose   tough as old boots

\   \

on show   inedible

/   /

mushroom - spread out   sawed-off

| \

swell   attacker   rifle

| /   \

mount - post - forward   search

| \

scale   maxilla - bill - hype - plug - keep your nose to the grindstone

| / |

bone up   power point   kit

| \ |

Estudios sencillos   draw attention to   tackle

| | |

guileless   dead heat   embark

| /

open - sweeping - across the board

|

blanket

/

bandage - swathe

|

compress - squash - cassava

b)rainstorms

The brain is 80% rain
- Louis Cabri

i)

rain is an electrochemical organ;
generating a hailstorm, or simply
interconnecting nerve cells discharged at one time.

scalp records of atmosphere as thunder
and its acoustic effect on activity emanating from
the rain. displayed in the form of rainwaves.
cloud type bulbs

when the rain is aroused and engaged in blown over activities, it
generates ocean waves. waves range from 15 to 40 cycles a second
& may line up in a nimbus or rainband, known as a squall line.

a person in active conversation would be in a layer of the troposphere
flows through the making of speech rotating supercells.

walks in the garden often inflicted by downburst winds.
greater amplitude and slower frequency
rising packet of air to cool less than its surrounding air
can't recall the last five miles, an instability is present in the
atmosphere.
the repetitious nature of clouds to form.

moisture is often free flow and occurs without censorship or guilt
an unstable air mass prone to a flow of ideas
a lifting force, a shower

attempting sleep as rain falls.
dreams melt to become consistent across cultures
as a downburst will descend from wind shear
contemplate anvil shapes of the forthcoming day

a state where dissipation becomes so automatic
that you can rapidly disengage from the atmosphere

dreamless, into liquid drops
vapour condenses, but never down to zero
            because that would mean that you were rain dead

ii)

damage: leaf shattering
and loss
effects of rainfall
shortage of oxygen
removing the highly digestible

damage: mercury

and its compounds on fields of cured alfalfa

damage: leaching is the movement
of cells that produce myelin
often assessed by the use of respiration,
and leaf loss
the breakdown
of soluble inability to process reality

damage: in serious cases of rain injury,
the result can be less substrate
for bacteria involved in the fermentation process

damage: common sense tells us that additional grey matter is lost.

damage: with each passing rainstorm
speech or movement problems shatter
after they die/dry
there may also be moisture changes
involving the inability
to separate daydream from memory

pressure within the skull can flood basements, rot cortical areas
set off mould growth in the dark areas of the hippocampus
lesions are the main structures that keep rainwater from entering
the alterations in cerebral blood flow

damage: listlessness, refusal to nurse
or eat rarely falls straight down
and the wind can easily push
water in through exposed
traumatic rain injury

damage: consider using a lithium treatment during the rainy season

(bruising of rain tissue), blood is mixed among tissue
soaking in through changes in sleep patterns

The mind of a man is a puddle in a rainstorm
- Robin Skelton

iii)

lightning is a lesson in humility.

activity of anchoring

and trafficking receptors

begin to rise

into the atmosphere
as points
where the membranes
of raindrops.
drops appear

to touch dendritic
spines

the small volume

of the cleft

still remains
elusive

absorbs heat

and changes
to a vapour

causes channels

to open that

are permeable

to higher temperature

why does the puddle dry up?

earth's gravitational

pull may

move quickly

enough
to break away

from the surface

of the liquid

and carry
heat away

in the form
of a vapour or gas.

a treated victim

away from its mother liquid

rvr vly

rvr vly (for Edmonton)

te
xt
i
nto
tex

ture

t n   prov
eh   i   oke
a   aw   n im me t
l   ret   o sw
o
ne
w
in the sun   i
im   ches flicker   Go   t
ages   as bran   ds   the h
beh   to walk along   pat
ind ey   me pur   wa
elids   su   ys
trigg   ade
er memo
ry to l
let t
he m
ice in
helpi
ng me
to eras
e my n
ame

currents

I do not limit myself: I imitate
many fancy things such as the dull red
cloth of literature, its mumbled griefs
- Lisa Robertson

thawing
vap
our
fav

fences of ambiguities
disarming toss

uttering lung
daunting   a   just   ment
eulogy.   gallop / tunnels
offer provoked range

opposing open-air
the affluent, safe
from smacks of upscale shame

gush
ing wo
n’t pith
courage
f)or plac
ing   clim(b)ax(e)
h   alt
     ing

drawn	to	cables
hot	like	vowels
tunnel	and	circle
come	to	tame
nouns	like	currents
eyes	and	tongues
left	to	dry
wilt	like	wishes
blown	and	scattered

turn tournailler turn tournailler turn tournailler turn tournailler turn tournailler
turn tournailler t**urn tour**nailler turn tournailler turn tournailler turn tournailler

polaris

bouquet stereo

lush stone

groomed

hear)t p a/u ddle

chase pur

set to ring merit
glazing sunk
occupying windows
replicating
blank
roots

slat plug
salt gulp

turn in to a p(l)ace of fragrance

viburnum spin(e
star sw|amp
awning over bustling flurry
                                    in certain circles

bonjour hello bonjour hello bonjour hello
bonjour hello bonjour hello bonjour hello
bonjour hello bonjour hello bonjour hello
bonjour hello bonjour hello bonjour hello
bonjour hello bonjour hello bonjour hello
bonjour hello bonjour hello bonjour hello
bonjour hello bonjour hello bonjour hello
bonjour hello bonj***our hell***o bonjour hello
bonjour hello bonjour hello bonjour hello

spark winter
grip of crippling surge

the ammunition in burgundy
maverick
attitude   L
                            melodies   defunct

sirius

ly(e

oracles go flat
fog will shift
verbs can drown
circuits go vacant
gravity will shift
static can knot

pipe chuckles

busting
                com
unicate
                        fleeting moments

brass stanzas
crack

undrum
             con
tinue

pocketing demands of
spotlight   s
yndr
ome
          the faith holds the attitude

paradigm shift
cordial* diminishing

* core dial
chord isle
cored deal

turning	in	grounds
solid	with	pleasure
seeking	for	tides
bound	in	knots
frayed	with	rhythm
lust	for	space
fields	in	winter
tripping	with	atmosphere
aesthetic	for	static
hissing	in	clouds
damp	with	diphthongs
uttering	for	volts
thrown	in	warmth
tides	with	crescents
pull	for	gravity

timbre stamp
timbre stamp
timb **rest** amp
timbre stamp
timbre stamp
timbre stamp
timbre stamp

c ve

ar\ra

season

sought mirror

morning signs

depth

knuckle flutter
on the verge of t)urning
verse

th
under
as

boreal sleep, the   s oil s pace
plethora cuts pivotal ampersands*
erasing argument treble clefs

p)itches increase trawlers depleting
in beige hunts for cotton

* amps per sand
ohms per soil
watts per dirt
volts per clay

pre-tension unparallel
harm
omi
zed   hope
in gestures and stains

i
gni
ti
on

neuron
near on
cir c um fr ance
/st

solution so loosen

s)our lexicon flanked //bet
ween// hairpin atlas
the rhythm of the pavement

outside	our	parameter
shocks	from	surge
beige	or	opal
seek	our	attention
away	from	speech
gust	or	wire

p
ending
b

the bitch in habitual

uninstalled

Erasure poems from Celines' *Death on the Installment Plan*

for Reg Johanson

again…I niche…Hell!
moving…I'm
while…There's

around…Down
from…I

water
…I
now…It's
far…Maybe
now…I
…I'm out…I'm
good…I'm in…So
move…
I'll Meanwhile…I
try…I back…There's
all…This
me…not
a thing…Just
myself
…Slowly station…I wrap

overcoat…I don't
recognise me
…I slide walls… I don't soul…
The open…good deal…I stretch
bench…There's a
near…I'm doing fine…I'm in the dark…The
first at five…I haven't
damn thing…It was
the bed
…To hell without it…I don't
there…it can't be done…the one
Scarce …I sit up
awake…I'm
train…I'm board…
I lie there… I

of it…My folks seem pleased
see me…They

point…they scenario…
They were
private wor-
ries…in the
deal…their whole appearance

72

engine of
a bellyache

surrounded by
tongues

swearing louder
juggled with splinters
the leaks
were marvellous

stank up the country side

let me speak more
softly

suffocating

A little hiccup. That's all.

measure everything

to the slaughterhouse

part of my sleep

temperature

union blackmail

single word in

brick shithouse

Nothing doing.
on the ground …

…

…

various noises

He must be alone

end! An arpeggio
perking up

next, sharp, cutting, bleeding in the light, streets blue, red,

buffeting the current

my concierge banging

can she be coming
so softly

She doesn’t

18

cornered

deep burns

miserable doll. Up and down she goes,

wheezing

"it makes

you piss"

On the sidewalk there's

a little dog with a limp.

Everything attaches itself to me today.

To play it absolutely
in the
-off places
In his bones,
digging in deeper
come to see us
so thrifty so
conked out

of cancer abstinence.

vacations.

ended up in

a village all own

shot
all flesh, desire, music,

take little liberties

31

crummy,
poetry

mercury.

And so on.

poor bastards
passing each other
remedies

of razor blades

timid little white collar

halfwits

That's our bread and butter.

point blank:

masterpiece?

Almost everyday

torn down

without money

a modest

racket in

something soft

people, I fuck around too much,

bursts into lamentations

the fruit of a promise

tight-lipped

We'd drink the horde of
lunatics

those feverish
cussing us out

humiliate me
out of a clear sky
I'll have to teach you something about
ellipses
one thing
solitary
little louse…

to ask you about the Zodiac and its signs?
head in both hands

such a revelation
couldn't stand it another
minute

down to more pressing

annotate

do you hear me?
go drop in

your own hook… …not a word

23

finer features

expect life to coddle them

jerk-off intellectual

good at telling yarns

84

, ’ ab-
solutely divine …
throbbing tits … ’ …
sheathed in an airy negligee … ’ , ’
sobbing … ,
… ‘ ,
…
… ‘
, … …

73

woolen

tantrum

plotting

corsets.

With his Santa Clause act

the words of an epic

half dosing

with the last glow of
daylight

rattles
shadows

moans

“Crushed beneath a heap of f lowers,
losing blood

arson hearts

noose paper

tunnel and circle preserving pranks and whispers
to satisfying scrapes
stopping glass clatter abundance. chop off
averse process. pressure instead.
                    the liar shall lie down/on the lam?

                                                                            gratifying soil
senses develop recluse desire. frame scandalous
windows.

                              stained throaty texture

                                                                            encompassing
current hinges crowd sound in temporary ounces.
messages of neglect gouging

                                                                            used
up all my pity

fall flawless in sabre sketch alouettes
roll onto season of wait in wings quote of prediction

basking in cross wire confidence

        ladder slip/strike out
steer words to open space

                    sentences de-feathered and skinned
                    your voice bellows ink stain thumbprint.

                              trigger.
inches of laughter.

joy riding emerald idea(l)on(g)

in the fray of a dirty word
draining. awash.
remedies for falsehood peeling layers
of star-skin
to filter pictures for guilt while your
vowels crack the frame

your text(ure) is rust on nails

arson hearts

blood brain / volume objecting to the sunlight pulsing
hesitation stimulate long saddle of morning
skin stretch to fuse coral departing of doubt
avenging filthy jokes where the rain comes in
jack-knifing to thumb spirit : poly vocal burn to
sense of whirly knots in amplifier hum

, evaporate

the alphabets of air asleep in the details
ratios…nil.   trade me yours

slumped waves shift to bench stubble
side winding | undressed   recalled dullness

import(ance) of shadows haunting fields

sweating glass
casting dappled
navigating
set best
neurons
built over

mark out
upper maps
stairways
eating thru
minutes

leaked diamond sentence our wounds
sky-ribs / perfume of your core, wailing. consume 'til our
atoms take over   distances drown out the slow
senseless taste with unannounced words and numerous
sound. becomes faun-like ruptured displacement

revelry scalp. branched thin language octaves we used
to shatter oak leaves to exhaust
unfriendly wishes lay in our bones and sinews

shot the linen deep

cyst humour.   discreet, ripples the yoke
my parables escape fists

rotation / nailed live tails / reacting / gnaw
weather resonance : emerges tin

rusting sounds of senile songs

offers of knives
in the soil
cut hint
of grass. drawn
circles and expose
roots. need of
showing air

turpentine dream
knots form nooses to wrap round hives of nitrate

stubborn nudges

mouth invites vanity

dismantle
places we kept soft

mongoloid paragraphs chance dampening colonies of
veins open door like a uterus. lavitities true
colours

citrine skin, lagoons

porcelain bond
    the poison set in... spokes in burnt umber
and pouty//. corner. losing ground

crumbling riverbank of blackboard equations
cluster trust as a compliment salvaging the
remains

badge cloud. remain over sleep patterns

dig fins revolve around vanilla (em)brace ovary
bust shores up your honesty

response for screening point cinder line

empties
-hooks,
immobilized
affable
torment

black
ripped
cast
spine
mask

onto
worry.
struggles
debut

______
cleaned,"
predictions
double over

before pile
symbol of
wrong.
curvature

arson hearts pounded curves into suckling stars

heritage mightened.encase and store all generating
veins eclipsing nameless texture

of our history?

Tremolo

Theatre, organ fat. thud. spilling into salas.
wound skill if screening;
.conduct. accommodate
cheat credence stance

criss-cross fodder

Treasure hunt seared spaces for additional   focus enmeshed and closing all the scars a skin
holds renunciation where there is no technique

shrugs of sacrificing samba (((((your gifts are exasperated weeds
a frustration in short speech your orchid strive for fickle heaves.
smoke impression blows umbrellaing chatter

prying compound
phosphorus
moon-clammy
trebling pouting palm   cascade countless pulse

odium or chains?

light gleam
in even mentor
my September, my Thoth.

lured
into bitter ribs
        fussing

a cataract guide to sawdust sons of mahogany shimmy.a chant sutured boundaries erratic static. stagnant smother to overcome soil.   voices wasp- sputter to smoke out spatial howl overbridging sodium reason. the focus will shift. pale, naked bulb

tape swells

(i)

cusp structured. reel in culture marble
seeping knee ; hold breath in
slacken dew. hold breath in boiling
nails. hold breath in honey angst to
conceal your engraved chorus of

pocketed scar.
hold
breath

(ii)

in
clapping
cloth.
hum
grip
for
yokes

of wire map.
ripple scratch,
fist break marrow
accordion glint. :font into valve
tolerance of touch

melts like /tar

on Irish

roads.

p u l .l
,,decision cord and sink into fits of skin

(iii)

habit escape rambling to spread on accord of incentives
in the palm. mitosis dream wax respectable. flutter on
lashes.
          hopscotch. saturated"wheeze{ nostalgia became
the ash you swept. bone taunt `^ achieved trace to
disappear through
                              thermal notes. chapped |.| slathered

illegible seasons

Discards from drafts of Rimbauds *A Season In Hell*

Bad Blood

resumes
the

grew
climbs felt to me
it's said
^ play
my hope [?] and my higher treasons and my
^

blows
^

I'll fight for
^
At

to avoid bruta[l] hand [?]
today, on the steps
the hard life
I won't grow old

To what end and my
How

[illegible word]
Do I know
Where, I go

they
move

The pack saddle

False Conversion

glass

My

the devil,

As one should

It's

a handsome and good

Satan well ^

salvation

As soon as

the apparition of thousands of charming people

I'll rebegin

The misfortune o my misfortune and the misfortune of others which matters little to me

animal life ^

still life still

We had the

the

the demon

When

I believe in hell so here I am

^

the th

the

So the poets are damned. No, that's not it.

Shut up.

it's

Alchemy of the word

[ ]
From London or Peking, or Ber[ ]
disappear joke on [ ]
Look [ ]
little [illegible] [ ]
wanted the chalky desert of [ ]

prayed to
and;
[*sic*]
pieces
spiders And [illegible word]

quickly burning boudois

I wore clothing made of [four illegible words]
The sun set towards the shit, at the centre of
the earth [three illegible words]
convulsion

dissolves in a sunbeam
and which will wilt in the sun

Hunger

I think about about animals
[illegible word], little
innocent
bodies the romantic spider made a romantic shadow
invaded by the opal dawn:
[illegible word]
for us to [illegible word]

from contact which I try

I believe I have found

I [several illegible words, crossed out]
from

I expressed *the most* stupidly.

Eternity

the crowning blow

Golden Age

period it was
worldly laws

came myse

not life bad
Instinctive only, me I
leave with knowledge, an devi-
ation genius
[ ]
[ ]
[ ]
[ ]
[ ]
[ ]
I could not repeat them all and others
hallucinations
and many others and others
I know how to do it
were [several illegible crossed-out words]

I believed
fled
more
sadder and more remote
horrifying no longer

Memory

demise

[...]

[...]

[...]

Ends of the earth

will shut my

will remember in

wanted to recognize the

[illegi-

ble phrase] the magic ting in the luminous water illuminated

clean of these aberrations

magics

my remorse I the world seems brand

new; to me who had the possible impressions;

only

[illegible crossed-out word]

very truly

matutinum

when for

the strong among Christ comes the

BL[IS]S

Pity
Such misfortune
^
[ence].
[illegible phrase]

My beauty [?]

about the author:

Robert Swereda is a member of the Filling Station collective in Calgary. He studied creative writing at Capilano University in Vancouver. Recent work has been published in *In Air/Air Out, Steel Bananas*, *CV2, The Enpipe Line Anthology, Poetry Is Dead,* and *Unwrapped: The Bareback Anthology.*

33936749R00076

Made in the USA
Charleston, SC
26 September 2014